The Cycle of Love:

The Stages of My Heart

Lashawn Jefferson

Shamone L. Publishing

New York

Published by

Shamone L. Publishing
New York, NY 11422

International Standard Book Number (ISBN)
paper: 978-0-6151-8181-3

Printed in the United States of America
4th printing

Dedication

This book is dedicated to my best friend, Regine who thinks love is overrated. And the men, who filled my desire, want and need, and taught me that love comes in different stages, thank you.

Acknowledgments

I want to thank my aunt for being my one true love and providing me with the essentials of life, which have allowed me to accomplish all my dreams along with being the wonderful person I am. I love you!!

Table of Contents

The Want 1

    Fully Assembled 2

    Quest for Love 3

    In the back... 4

The Love...5

    So in Love..6

    Out of Control 7

    LOVE 8

    Trying...9

    What it Craves 10

    All I Need 11

    Ocean's Wave 12

The Struggle...13

    Once Doubted..14

    Fool for Love 15

    Is It Enough?!..16

    Will We Survive?!? 17

    So Many Questions 18

    For the Love..19

    If I'm that... 20

The Heartbreak 21

    How..22

    Dear God, ...23

    Across from Me 24

The Recovery 25

    Consumed 26

As I grab the sheets...27

Surprised..29

What I would do 30

The Want

Fully Assembled

Don't want a man to complete me for I am already whole

I want a man to be mine for the taking

I want him to be a part of my life for what it is

I want him to be my inspiration

I don't want a man to complete me for

I am already whole

I want a man to be complete in him self

For I want him

for the taking

I'm fully assembled before I get there

I'm not trying to raise a boy into a man

For I am a woman fully assembled before you got here.

I want him to cater to me for

I don't want a man to complete me for

I've come fully assembled

I want a man that's there for the taking

Quest for Love

Why is it that we know that no one can love us better than

we can love

ourselves,

yet

we spend most of lives looking for

someone

to

love

us

as much as we

desire,

want,

need

and

deserve

The funny thing about life is

no one ever

gets what they

desire,

need,

want

and

deserve all at the same time.

So where does that leave us

and

our quest for love?

In the back...

In the back of my heart it sits there waiting to be released.

I'm holding back,

Not letting myself go.

Not letting you love me. I'm afraid of being hurt, afraid of letting go.

What happens

If you stop loving me or have a change of heart?

What happens

If I don't love you,

What happens

If I run and you don't chase.

What happens if you leave and I stay?

In the back of my heart it sits and waits for the moment I let go and you

start loving me.

Can you be what my dreams are made of or is it just a dream.

Will you ever love me enough to stop loving me.

Will I every love you enough to let go.

In the back of my heart it sits and waits for me to let go.

The Love

So in Love

I've been feeling like something has come over me like a peace

inside. When I'm with you the world stops

nothing matters but you.

I can't and won't stop loving you.

I'm loving always

and I hope it won't be in vain don't break my heart don't

send me away crying.

Just love me. Just hold me until life stops.

I want to live in your arms I want to feel this way til I fall asleep.

I want to just love you.

But I'm afraid.....

To let go and just love always.

I'm afraid to just love...

you,

are u?

Out of Control

How you make me feel is unexplainable.

I adore the way u kiss me.

How your heart beats faster when I lay next to you.

I miss the way you make me feel, how easily you bring tears to

my

eyes.

How crazy it is that you can talk about a million chicks

yet

I know that your heart is mine & no one elses.

I miss us, I miss being the one & only.

But as great as it feels

I hate the feeling

I get when you leave

how much the pain stays

&

that makes me withdraw that makes me

shutdown.

How did I get here

&

why do I keep doing it to myself.

I'm so out of control.

LOVE

I love you more than words can describe.

It's hard to explain to others why and how but I just do.

I know things can be hard at times and confusing even more of the
time.

What I know for a fact is that I love you with all my heart and whether I
will admit it or not I only want
to be with you.

I can see myself waking and finding you on the floor next to me
(LOL)   forever, which is a very long time

With or without the titles you are my baby, my everything, and
we have a working understanding at this time.

So I just wanted to let you know!

Love you always and forever.

Trying....

Trying

to find that piece of mind.

Trying

to let go yet hang on all at the same time,

Losing grip but still holding tight.

Trying

to pretend not to care

Trying

to love on instinct.

Trying

to live off the words you do and don't say.

Trying

to love what's left.

Trying

to keep my cool while being so hot.

Trying

to kiss you while wanting to fuck you.

Trying

to find what once was,

now.

What it Craves

What my body craves is only you.

What is hard to explain is why???

I can be kissed by anyone but my lips only want yours...

I can be touched by many but my body needs yours.....

I need to hear you say you love me

I need you to tell me you are right here

I need you to make love to me for my body craves it.....

Only you can satisfy my body cravings....

My body craves your love, your touch, your kiss.....

My body craves for YOU!!

And that's hard for me to explain why but

I DO!

All I Need

All I need is you

your smile

your touch,

your love

Without it, I'm just not complete....

What is it that you need?

Do you need me?

Do you still want me?

Cause it seems that I'm not all you need

Ocean's Wave

Understand that
I love you.
How much you mean to me.
You complete me, which I don't mind.
My world started
when you
became my man.
My life had meaning when
I started to love you.
So before I put my heart on ice until it's needed.
I need you to know how much you really mean to me
How much this love we got means to me
Some people don't get how
and
why I'm so weak for you.
Why I wait for you but I don't care.
I know what love is and it's you and me.
And I don't care what it takes this love will conquer all
You can etch that in stone
Loving you always and forever.
Waiting patiently
with
love as strong
as the
oceans wave.

The Struggle

Once Doubted

Once doubted I'm no longer the same....

You doubted what we had and who I am

Now I see you as just another...

You doubted our love

What we had

What we were

Now I see things with you, as cloudy as I did with him.....

you are all the same....

got the best but looking for better knowing it don't get no BETTER!

Fool for Love

Here I am making a fool of myself by loving you yet and still. Why I
don't know and how I can't figure out yet I am.
I have what I want yet I don't have what I need.
Do I hurt the one who loves me, for the love that hurt me.
The irony of life is that it is what it is, how I can't get over my past to
move on with my future.
I'm just made out to be a fool for love.
So I just live with my choices for they are my own
my mistakes my actions
my consequences

Is It Enough?!

Do u ever feel that whatever u do,

isn't good enough,

even if it's everything they ask of u?

No matter how hard u try,

they always see what u fall short of?

U know why right?

Cuz it's not good enough.

There will be a day when no matter what u do,

you won't be appreciated.

Maybe one day,

whatever I do,

will be enough,

especially when whatever I'm doing is more than u ever had.

Just maybe,

maybe one day,

my not enough is better than not at all,

when u never had.

Lol...what the hell am I thinking,

what world am I living in?

U know the song,

"Almost doesn't count",

that's real talk.

Maybe whatever I do,

will never be enough.

Will We Survive?!?

There are things about love people don't understand.

There are things about life no one gets.

But we work with want we got.

We make things work when we have to.

There are things in life we deal with

because we have to

because we want to.

Things are hard for so long we wonder when they will become easy.

Things become so filled that we don't stop to enjoy life.

I wonder why things are so hard why things are so

complicated

when they don't have to be.

Why can't life be easy?

Why can't we love without emotions?

Why must things have reason why must we live?

If life was easy would we want to live would we want to cry at that! Life

is hard not because we make it,

it's because it has to be

without it being hard how will we learn.

How will we love so deep!?

How will we survive?

So Many Questions

How could a love so strong no longer exist?

How could a I love so deep now be so shallow?

How can a person so open love a person so closed?

Why does love play with my heart and mind?

All I needed was a kiss to feel loved, now I need more.

How can one take three steps forward and four steps back?

Do you not want me?

Do you not want this to work?

Do you no longer want this to work?

Do you love her?

Do you want her?

Do you need her like you needed me?

Do you touch and kiss her like you do me?

Do I care that you do?

Do you care that I know more than what you say?

Would you tell me if you did?

Would I believe it?

My mind has so many questions yet no answers.

Could I ask the questions I really don't want to know the answers to?

Do I want to know?

Do I need to know?

Will you answer the questions?

Will you tell me what I really don't want to know?

Or just what I want to know?

When will I know?

For the Love...

Love is suppose to be forever,

A once in a lifetime thing.

Your suppose to live happily ever after right?

What happens when you don't love forever

When you lose hope and your ability to love

What happens when you no longer can love

When loving isn't enough

When love is just another thing or person

You can't love forever its impossible, right?

What happens when you stop loving after so long

When you stop being the one being loved or the one loving.

What happens when the kisses aren't sweet.

When the touch isn't the same but just another.

What happens when your heart stops beating....

for the love?!?

If I'm that...

If I'm that great...if you love me that much...if I'm exactly what you've been looking for....if I'm everything...then why am I here....why can't you give up your fears...why can't you just love and be with only me....I guess you just don't love me that much.....I guess I'm just not worth that much........so let the pain begin and life continue as it is......

The Heartbreak

How...

I'm not sure how to feel or where to run.

I thought I would be ok. I thought it would go away.

When I'm near you now I quiver.

When I close my eyes I see you with her doing the same.

I have vision of that night with him.

Wishing I could take it all back.

Wishing I can start all over make it all disappear,

how am I suppose to feel where do I go from here,

how much more can I stand.

Is this love or a desire for it.

When I look in the mirror I don't see me.

When did I lose myself when did I change

When did I become crazy in love with you and why and how.

Do you run or stay?

Do I cry in the darkness wishing it all away,

wishing I could turn back time and never be in love?

How do you mend a broken heart with tape without tears without

regret!

How do I move on.

Do I just love you without words without expression without care?

Where can I hide away...will you be there trying to get away!?

Or do I just hope and cry in darkness wishing for the

good

over

the bad.

Dear God,

This is poem dedicated to Iris

Remember me. I'm the one who asked for the chance to love; now I'm asking for you to take it back. I know love is hard and doesn't come easy but this is too much. I didn't expect to still be crying myself to sleep every night. I just want a return; I want back my heart from before it wasn't all that bad. I tried it your way. I tried being patient, kind and understanding but I've gotten no where. I didn't expect it to be this hard. I sometimes wonder why you let me live cause if this is the reason you should have let me cut deeper before and taken me out of my misery then. I haven't asked for much so maybe it is just me. Maybe I'm not supposed to love or be loved. I just want peace. I need you to take back the love I asked for or give me a sharper knife next time. I need a repair on my heart its broken into so many places by so many people. Can you please just repair what's done and let me love no more, please. I know you should not ask for what you can't handle but I thought I could and I really did try, I tired over and over. Just undo what's been done so I can start all over and continue to cry myself to sleep at night wanting the chance to be loved and love. I guess I should be careful what I ask for or I just might get it, again!

Across from Me

as I
sit on the bus and look across the way
I
make
eye contact
with a young lady about my age when
our eyes
meets we get lost in them
what we see is amazing cause we can't believe
someone else
has that same painful look we see in ourselves
I
can see the hurt and disappointment in her eyes
I
can see the years of pain and wondering what if and why
what's there is familiar to me cause that's exactly how
I
feel what's
so difficult
to understand is that
someone is going through it too.....

The Recovery

Consumed

There was a time when love consumed me,
it was
my everything
I lived and died for that love.
But the love wasn't returned.
The same love that consumed me, gave me the
greatest happiness
on earth yet caused me the
greatest pain of my life,
a pain I never want to feel again.
So now I'm consumed with the downfall of that love.
So now everything I do is to
prevent me from never ever being
consumed by a love that strong.
For love didn't
kill me
but left a
scar
that reminds me why I will
never love again.

As I grab the sheets

I lay there in the dark I feel you reach for me.

As you caress my body with your sweet touch.

Then you spread my legs

and

kiss my lips

you caress my clit with your tongue

I grip the sheets

and

bite my bottom lip to

shadow the sounds of my moans

you reach for me

then

caress my breast with your mouth slowly

and

entering me with your fingers to caress my inner walls.

I grip the sheets and bite my bottom lip to shadow my moans.

You then tease me with your dick slowly touching my walls

and

kissing my neck whispering in my ear

asking me if I want you and me answering yes.

You enter me slowly I grip the sheets

and

bite my bottom lip to shadow my moans.

You move slowly making sure I feel every motion of you inside of me.

Feelings so good that I have to grip the sheets

and

bite my bottom lip to shadow my moans.

Then you kiss my neck to go with the motion of your hips

then

whisper in my ear do I love you

and

I say yes then you ask me do I like it and I say yes.

As I climax I can no longer shadow my moans by gripping the sheets

and

biting my bottom lip.

As I moan loudly my alarm goes off.

Was it a dream or my body screaming really loud?

Surprised

surprised myself today with a thought of you.

remembering how you kissed, touched and caressed me

it felt real

I desired you for a little while wanting to get that last

passionate

love making we had

How surprised I was when

I awoke.

What I would do

What I would pay to touch

your body

What I would give

to kiss your lips

What I would give to feel you inside of me,

saying my name

The things I would give to have that

one wish

what I would give and pay

but

I can't...

About the Author

Lashawn currently lives in New York where she is working full-time and studying to get her MBA from Ellis College. Lashawn's been writing since she was a teenage and expresses her life's ups and downs in her writing. She hopes to publish more books because writing is her great escape.

Page Left Blank

Page Left Blank

Page Left Blank

Page Left Blank

Page Left Blank